Through the Rainbow

THEY WERE BRAVE

Silver Book 6

by E. S. Bradburne

Illustrated by W. M. Ireland

SCHOFIELD & SIMS LTD HUDDERSFIELD

0 7217 0228 7
0 7217 0237 6 Net Edition

First Impression 1971
Second Impression 1972
Third Impression 1972
Fourth Impression 1973

Printed in Scotland by McFarlane & Erskine Ltd.
Bound in Scotland

Contents

Theseus and the Minotaur

On the island of Crete there stood a great palace. Below the palace was a maze of dark passages in which lived a terrible monster with the head of a bull. It was called the Minotaur.

Every nine years the King of Crete, whose name was Minos, sent a message across the sea to the people of Athens. Seven young men and seven maidens were to be sent to Crete to be given to the Minotaur to eat.

Now there was a brave young man, the son of the King of Athens, whose name was Theseus. When he heard about King Minos' dreadful demand he offered to go himself, as one of the seven young men.

At last the seven men and seven maidens were chosen. Their mothers gave them food for the voyage and told them stories of brave men to help them to face the dreadful adventure in front of them. Then they went on to the ship that was to take them to the island of Crete. Sadly their mothers and fathers said farewell to them and away they sailed.

Soon a great storm arose, but at last they reached the island and there was King Minos himself to count them. The young men and maidens were taken to the palace, guarded by soldiers.

That night Theseus slipped away from the guards. His plan was to find the Minotaur and kill it. But how could he find his way among the maze of passages below the palace? And when at last he found it, how would he be able to kill so strong and dreadful a monster? And if he were able to kill it, how could he and his friends make their escape from the island?

Help was near at hand. King Minos had a daughter, named Ariadne, who, as soon as she saw Theseus, fell in love with him. Ariadne wanted, more than anything, to save Theseus from being eaten by the Minotaur.

That night when all was dark and silent she crept out of the palace and followed Theseus. She whispered to him that she was going to help him and then she gave him a ball of thread.

"Tie this to the doorpost," she said. "And let it unroll as you go along the passages. You will find the Minotaur sleeping in the darkness. You must take it by the hair and kill it. You will be able to find your way back by following the thread. I will be waiting here for you when you return."

Theseus took the ball of thread and tied one end to the doorpost at the entrance to the maze. Then in he went, feeling his way along the dark passages that twisted and turned, first this way and then that.

Now he was quite alone. He could hear nothing but the beating of his own heart and the drip of water from the rock above his head.

Suddenly he heard a sound of something moving. He stood still and listened, holding his breath. Then on he crept into the darkness. The Minotaur must be somewhere just ahead.

The sounds grew nearer, a noise of tramping feet and loud breathing. A strange animal smell came towards him. Theseus turned a corner and suddenly there was the Minotaur in front of him, a huge monster, its body all covered with hair and on its bull's head, two great horns.

Theseus remembered what Ariadne had told him and made a grab to take it by the hair. There was a great struggle, for the Minotaur was mighty and strong, but Theseus held on and at last he gave it a great blow and killed it.

Theseus found his way back through the maze of passages, leaving the dead Minotaur behind him. At last he came to the entrance, and there was Ariadne awaiting him.

"Quick," he said, "we must go down to the ship."

In the meantime his friends, too, had escaped from the soldiers and together they found their way to where the ship lay waiting. Quickly they rowed away,

but they had hardly left the island when they saw some ships following them. In the darkness they fought a battle. The ships were beaten off and Theseus and his friends made their escape and came at last to Athens.

The people of Athens were overjoyed to see them return in safety. They feasted and danced and sang in praise of brave Theseus. Never more would their sons and daughters be sent on the dreadful voyage to the island of Crete, for the Minotaur was dead at last.

Daniel and the Lions

Once a young man named Daniel was taken prisoner and carried off into a land far from his home. Here, although he was a prisoner, he was taken to the Royal Palace to wait on the King.

One night the King had a dream which troubled him very much. He wanted to know what it meant and so he sent for his Wise Men.

"I have had a dream," he said to them. "If you do not tell me what my dream was, and what it meant, you shall be torn in pieces."

But none of the Wise Men could tell the King what his dream meant, and at this the King lost his temper and in a great rage ordered that they should all be put to death, and Daniel was to die with them.

When the captain of the King's bodyguard came to put the Wise Men to death, Daniel asked him why the King had made such a cruel order. When Daniel heard what the King had said he went to him and begged that he would wait a little time before he had the Wise Men put to death.

Then Daniel went home and asked God to help him. He prayed all night and before morning he knew what he must say to the King about the meaning of his dream.

When the King heard what Daniel had to say and how much wiser he was than his own Wise Men he made him ruler over the land.

Daniel ruled well and wisely for many years until at last the King died. In time another King, named Darius, came to the throne, and now some of the other rulers of the Kingdom were jealous of Daniel and they tried to think of a plan to get rid of him.

They knew that King Darius would not believe them if they said that Daniel was not a good ruler, for everyone knew how good and wise he was. At last they thought of another way by which they could get rid of him.

They knew that Daniel prayed to God and that nothing would ever stop him from doing this, so they made a law that for the next thirty days no one was to pray to anyone except the King. The punishment for anyone who did not obey this law was that he should be thrown into a den of lions. They took the law to King Darius and asked him to put his name to it, for when he had done this, the law could never be changed. They knew that Daniel would never obey such a law and in this way they hoped they would trap him.

Everything turned out as they had planned. Daniel took no notice of the law, for nothing would stop him from praying to God, even with such a punishment waiting for him. When the men saw him praying, as he always did, they went and told the King that Daniel would not obey the law.

Darius was sorry when he heard this, but now that he had put his name to it, the law could never be changed and Daniel was taken and put into the den with the lions. A great stone was put at the opening of the den and King Darius himself sealed it with his own seal so that no one could go in and rescue Daniel.

Darius was so troubled that night that he could eat nothing and he could not sleep.

As soon as it was light, he arose and went to the lions' den. Standing by the great stone he called to Daniel.

"Daniel, servant of the living God, has your God

been able to save you from the lions?"

Then spoke Daniel, from inside the den, "Long live the King! My God sent his angel to shut the lions' mouths so that they have done me no harm."

When the King heard this he was full of joy and he gave orders for Daniel to be taken out of the den. The stone was rolled away and out came Daniel, quite unhurt. Then Darius told all his people that from now on they were to trust and believe in Daniel's God.

"For", said Darius, "He is the living God who has saved Daniel from the power of the lions."

The Gorgon's Head

There was once a wicked King who was always fighting with his brother. This King had an only daughter and he was told that in time she would have a son and by this son's hand he would die. When the King heard this he locked his daughter away in a dungeon with doors of brass. But she did, at last, have a baby. When the King found out he put her and the baby into a great chest and cast it into the sea.

Away floated the chest across the water until it came to the shores of an island. There a fisherman, walking along the beach, saw the strange chest and wondered what it could be. He waded out and threw his net over it and hauled it out of the sea.

Imagine his surprise when he found the King's daughter and her baby son inside it, both still alive. What was he to do with them, he wondered?

The fisherman had a brother named Polydectes. He was the King of the island and the fisherman took the mother and baby to his Palace.

The baby was named Perseus and in time he grew up to be a fine, strong, young man.

Polydectes, in the meantime, made up his mind that he would marry Perseus' mother, although she did not wish to marry him. Polydectes knew that as long as Perseus was alive he would never get his way, so he thought of a cunning plan to get rid of him.

He called his friends together and told them that he was going to marry someone else and asked each of them to give him a horse as a gift for his bride.

Perseus was very glad when he heard Polydectes say this and he believed that now his mother would be safe, so he said to Polydectes,

"I have no horse, nor any gold to buy one, but if you are not going to marry my mother I promise to win whatever gift you name, even the Gorgon Medusa's head, if need be."

Now, the Gorgon Medusa was a terrible creature. Her head was covered with serpents instead of hair and she was so ugly that all who saw her face turned to stone.

Polydectes was delighted when he heard the rash promise that Perseus had made, for he believed that Perseus would never return from such an adventure. He said to Perseus,

"The Gorgon's head would indeed please me more than any horse in the world." Perseus, having made his promise, realized that there was no way out.

At once he left Polydectes' Palace, to set out on his dangerous adventure. He had not gone far when, suddenly, there was a flash of light and there appeared in front of him a tall and beautiful lady. In one hand she carried a spear and in the other a shield, and on her head she wore a helmet.

Her clear grey eyes looked straight at Perseus, as she spoke.

"I am the Goddess of Wisdom," she said to him. "I help all who are brave and true. I know the task you have taken upon yourself and I have come to help you."

Then she held out her shield to him. Perseus covered

his eyes, for the shield was so bright that the light flashed from it as if from a mirror.

"Take this," said the Goddess. "It will save you when you go to slay the Gorgon. You must not look at her or you will be turned to stone. But if you hold this shield above your head you will see Medusa as though in a mirror. Then you can strike at her and slay her without looking at her."

At this there was another flash of light, and there, beside the Goddess, stood a beautiful youth.

"I, too, have come to help you," he said, and he handed Perseus a sword.

"Take this," he said. "It is strong enough to cut off Medusa's head." Perseus thanked them both for their gifts and then he said,

"But how am I to find Medusa? I know not where she dwells."

"You have a long journey before you," said the Goddess of Wisdom, "and there are more things you must have to help you on your way. You must find a pair of winged sandals to carry you across the oceans to the land where Medusa dwells. You must have the helmet of darkness which will make you invisible and the magic wallet in which you must put Medusa's head. These are all guarded by the Nymphs of Stygia. You must find your way to them and ask them for all these things."

"And where shall I find these Nymphs who can give me the sandals and the helmet and the magic wallet?" asked Perseus.

"Only the Gorgon's sisters know where the Nymphs are," said the goddess.

Perseus at once set off to seek for the Gorgon's sisters to ask them where he could find the Nymphs of Stygia.

At last, after many long days of weary journeying he came upon the Gorgon's sisters. These three dreadful creatures had only one eye and one tooth between them, and when Perseus came upon them they were passing the one eye and the one tooth from one to another.

Perseus crept up behind them, and quick as a flash he snatched the eye and the tooth from their hands.

"Ha!" he cried, "I have your eye and your tooth, and I will not give them back until you tell me where I can find the Nymphs of Stygia who guard the winged sandals, the helmet of darkness and the magic wallet that I must have for my adventure."

When the Gorgon's sisters knew they had lost their eye and their tooth they were forced to tell him what he wanted to know. Then away went Perseus to the far land of Stygia where the Nymphs lived.

When the Nymphs heard Perseus' story they begged him to stay with them and to go no further. But Perseus would not stay and so they gave him the sandals and the helmet and the magic wallet.

With the winged sandals on his feet Perseus was able to fly across the ocean far to the west, and here at last he found Medusa, lying asleep. All around her lay great rocks, worn by the rain, and, as Perseus looked at them, he saw that they were men and beasts that had turned to stone.

With the sword in one hand and the shield in the other Perseus rose in the air over the terrible sleeping Gorgon. Then, turning his face away so that he should not look into her eyes, he held the bright polished shield above his head, and looked at it. Then, as in a mirror he saw her, and with one stroke of the sword he cut off her head.

Still with his eyes turned away he thrust the head into the magic wallet and finally, wearing the helmet of darkness which made him invisible, he made his escape.

On and on he flew until, at last, as the sun was setting, he came to the palace of the giant Atlas, who held up the sky. As he flew past he opened the magic wallet and held up the Gorgon's head. When Atlas saw it he at once turned into a great mountain of stone, and there he stands to this day.

Perseus then flew onwards, across a great desert, and as he went, some drops of the Gorgon's blood fell on to the sand and turned into poisonous snakes.

And now he found himself flying along a sea coast, where huge cliffs stood. Here he saw a strange sight. Chained to a rock was a beautiful maiden. Perseus flew down and alighted close to her on the cliff. At once he fell in love with her.

This was Andromeda and here she had been left to

be eaten by a dreadful sea monster.

As Perseus watched, he saw the monster coming like a great ship through the waves, making straight for Andromeda. At once he rose in the air, drew his sword and dived, cutting off its head with one swift stroke.

When the monster was dead, Perseus took Andromeda to be his wife. Suddenly in the middle of the wedding there was a great noise and in dashed a band of armed men. At their head was a man who had planned to marry Andromeda himself.

A great fight took place until Perseus, seeing how many were against him, lifted up the Gorgon's head and turned them all to stone.

Then Perseus, taking Andromeda with him, returned to the island where he had left his mother. Here he found Polydectes feasting in the Palace. Perseus burst in and held the Gorgon's head aloft and all of them were at once turned to stone.

At last Polydectes was dead and Perseus was able to take his mother home to her own land. Before leaving he called the good fisherman, Polydectes' brother, to the Palace and made him King of the island in his brother's place. And so, at last, with his wife, Andromeda, and his mother, Perseus set sail for his own country. For many a day they sailed, and at last his boat came to the shore and Perseus made his way to the town. There the people told him that his grandfather, the King, had fled to another country.

But the wicked King could not escape his fate. The old story tells that Perseus followed him to this country and there he took part in the games that were being held, running and leaping and throwing the spear and the quoits. Perseus was better than anyone else in the games, for he was strong and swift and could run faster and throw the spear farther than anyone else.

At last came the final contest. This was throwing the quoit, a round flat circle of stone. Perseus took the first quoit and threw it far beyond all the rest, and the second also. As he reached for the last one he looked up.

There, on a throne hung with crimson silk, sat his grandfather watching. Perseus bent down and picked up the last quoit. With all his might he threw it, while the crowd cheered. Then, without warning, a gust of wind blew in from the sea, caught the quoit and blew it straight towards the throne where the King, Perseus' grandfather was sitting. It struck him on the foot, and with a cry of pain, the old man fell dead.

When the people knew who Perseus was, they made him King in his grandfather's place and he and Andromeda ruled the land for many long years.

When at last they died, the story tells, they were taken up into the sky, and there you may still see them on starry nights, Perseus holding the Gorgon's head and Andromeda stretching out her arms as Perseus first saw her, chained to the rock, waiting for the dreadful sea monster.

The Escape of the Little Duke

Richard, Duke of Normandy, was held prisoner in a castle of the King of France.

When he was only eight years old his father had been killed. The King of France had taken the boy away from his home in Normandy to live in the French castle. He was never allowed to go out nor to see any of his own people. He had one faithful companion, named Osmond, who watched over him day and night.

One day Richard and the King's youngest son were in the courtyard, playing ball. The great gate of the castle was closed and guarded by armed men. Suddenly Richard heard a voice outside. He ran to the gate and, standing on tiptoe, he looked through the small barred window. There, outside, stood a man dressed in a long dark robe, with a hood over his head, a staff in his hand, and sandals on his feet.

"It is a pilgrim!" called the King's son. "Let him in, guard. He shall be fed and rested."

"Blessings on you, young Prince," said the pilgrim, as the guard swung open the gate and let him in.

"It is a Norman!" cried Richard when he heard his voice. "You are from Normandy, are you not?" he said to the pilgrim. Then, to Osmond, "Osmond, Osmond, he comes from home, from Normandy."

The pilgrim went down on one knee and took the hand of the Little Duke. As he did so his hood fell back, showing his face.

"Why!" cried Richard. "It is Walter the huntsman!"

At this moment the King's oldest son Lothaire appeared.

"Who is this?" he cried.

"It is a Norman pilgrim," said his brother.

"He is no pilgrim," called Lothaire. "He is a spy

and a Norman dog. He shall be beaten. Away with him!"

"He shall not be beaten!" cried Richard, leaping up and throwing himself in front of the pilgrim.

The whip that had been meant for Walter, came down across Richard's neck, making a long red mark.

"My Lord Duke!" cried Walter.

Richard had snatched the whip from the hand of the guard. "Away! away!" he cried to Walter. "Make haste! Run! Run!"

Walter, knowing he could do nothing to help his young master, jumped to his feet, and ran as fast as he could through the castle gate and away.

Lothaire had been right. Walter was no pilgrim. He had come to find out what was happening to his master, the Little Duke, and in the hope that he might speak with Osmond. Now he hastened back to Normandy to tell what he had seen.

When the people of Normandy heard the story that Walter had to tell they were full of sorrow. For three days they ate nothing and everybody in the land, from the greatest to the least, went to church and prayed that God would save their Little Duke and bring him safely home.

Meanwhile, in the French castle, an even closer guard was kept on Richard. Osmond, knowing the danger he was in, tried to think of a way of escape, and at last he thought of a plan.

Late one evening, he came to Richard's room, carrying on his shoulders a huge bundle of straw.

"What is this?" asked Richard.

"What would you say, my Lord," said Osmond, "if we were to be in Normandy by tomorrow night?"

"In Normandy!" cried Richard. "Oh, Osmond, shall we really go? Has the King set me free?"

"Quiet," said Osmond. "Do just as I say, and you may yet be free."

Richard watched while Osmond fixed his sword into his belt. Then he gave the boy his dagger and

put some food in a leather bag. He wrapped Richard in a purple cloak and told him to lie down on the straw.

"We have to pass through the hall," he said. "I shall carry you out in this straw as though I was going to feed my horse, but you must be quite still and make no sound or all will be lost."

Richard promised to do exactly as Osmond told him. He lay down on the straw while Osmond pulled it round him so that he could not be seen.

"Remember, quite still. You must not move or rustle the straw," he said. "Now, are you ready?"

"I am ready," came Richard's voice from inside

the bundle.

He heard Osmond open the door, then felt him lift him up onto his back. Down the stone stairs they went and into the lighted hall, where the French men-at-arms were all feasting and talking.

Someone called out, "Do you go to feed your horse, Osmond?"

"Yes," replied Osmond, as he made his way carefully past the long tables carrying the huge bundle.

Richard held his breath as he felt the straw brushing against the tables. Would someone stop them before they could reach the door?

It seemed a very long time before he felt Osmond lift the latch of the door. Then it was dark again and Richard knew they were outside in the courtyard. Now Osmond's steps sounded on the flagstones and in a few moments they were in the stable.

Richard could hear the horses moving about in their stalls, but still he dare not speak nor move. Now he felt Osmond take him and put him over the saddle of one of the horses.

Holding him on by one hand, Osmond led the horse out of the stable. In a moment Richard heard the sound of its hooves on the wooden planks of the drawbridge.

In another moment they were over it and then, just as Richard felt he could bear it no longer, Osmond let him slide to the ground and onto his feet.

The straw fell away from him and Richard looked around. They were in a little wood. Above him the stars were shining in the dark sky and all was still and silent.

"We are free!" cried Richard. "Free, at last!"

"Not yet," said Osmond. "We are not free until we have crossed the river into Normandy. Up into the saddle, my Lord. We must ride for our lives."

He helped the Little Duke onto the horse, then mounted behind him. All night they rode and all the next day until at last they came to a wide river and beyond they saw a great castle.

"See!" called Osmond. "There lies your dukedom. There lies Normandy!"

But the danger was not yet over. The river was wide and swift and somehow they had to cross to the other side.

Osmond rode along the bank until they came to a place where the water was less deep. He slipped down from the saddle and waded into the water, leading the horse and holding Richard on its back.

Soon the water was up to Richard's feet, then over his knees and up over the horse's back. Now the horse started to swim and Osmond swam in front, holding the bridle.

At last he felt the ground under his feet, the water became shallower and less swift and they pressed towards the bank.

They were just scrambling out when they heard a voice from the castle walls above them.

"Hold! Who goes there?"

They looked up to see two men with their bows aimed straight at them.

"Bertrand!" cried Osmond. "Open the gates quickly!"

"Who calls me by my name?" called one of the

bowmen.

"It is I, Osmond, with your Duke, Richard, come home at last. Open the gates and let us in!"

"The Duke!" cried Bertrand, as he hurried down from the walls.

In a moment the gates were thrown open and to the cheers and shouts of welcome of a great crowd Richard rode into the courtyard of the Norman Castle, safely back in Normandy at last.

The Lord of Lorn

Long ago in Scotland there lived a Lord and his wife who had an only son.

When he went to school he learned more in one day than other children did in three. Soon he had learned all that his schoolmaster could teach him, so one day he mounted his horse and rode home.

"There is not a book in Scotland that I cannot read," he told his father.

When he heard this, his father made up his mind to send the boy to France in the care of the Head Steward. Before they set out his mother sent for the Steward and gave him a thousand pounds.

"Be good to my child in that far country," she said.

The Steward replied. "My lady, if I do him wrong then may God do the same to me."

But as soon as they landed in France the Steward began to treat the boy most unkindly. He gave him no food or drink and no money to spend.

One day the boy was so thirsty that he went down to the river bank to drink. While he was kneeling down beside the water the wicked Steward came up behind him and pushed him in.

The child cried out for mercy.

"Promise me you will give me all you have," said the Steward. When the boy had promised, the Steward pulled him out and made him take off his silk shirt and his fine clothes. Then the Steward gave him an old rough coat and sent him away up the hill to the house of a shepherd.

"You are no longer Lord of Lorn," said the Steward. "All you have belongs now to me."

The shepherd and his wife took in the young Lord of Lorn, not knowing who he was. They brought him up as their own son and every day he went out onto the hillsides to look after the sheep.

Meanwhile the wicked Steward used the thousand pounds to buy himself some fine clothes and then, calling himself the Lord of Lorn, he went to seek the hand of a Duke's daughter in marriage.

The Duke thought the Steward was a fine man and fit to marry his daughter so he made a great feast and promised to give him a thousand pounds a year when they were wedded.

Next day the Duke's daughter went out hunting. A hundred of the Duke's men went with her and they rode over hill and dale all day.

At last they came to the hillside where the young Lord of Lorn was keeping the sheep. He was sitting on the grass, crying to himself and when the Duke's daughter saw him she called her maid.

"Go fetch me the shepherd's boy," she said. "We will find out why he is crying so bitterly."

When the young Lord of Lorn was brought before her, the Duke's daughter asked him,

"Who are you, and why do you cry so bitterly? Do you not know that the Lord of Lorn is going to marry me?"

"Indeed," said the real Lord of Lorn, "I know him well. He is a brave Lord in his own country."

Then the Duke's daughter asked the boy if he would come and serve her, and this he willingly agreed to do, but when the Steward saw him he was very angry and pretended not to know him.

"Where were you born, you vagabond?" he said.

Then to the Duke's daughter he said,

"This boy's father robbed three thousand men in Scotland, far beyond the sea."

But the Duke's daughter did not listen to him and the young Lord of Lorn was sent to the stables to look after the horses.

For a year he worked in the stable taking good care of the horses, until one day when he was leading one of them to water, it suddenly lifted its head and hit him above the eye.

The pain made him cry out, and when the Duke's daughter heard him cry she ran to comfort him and make him well again.

"Tell me," she said, "tell me all your story."

"I cannot tell you," said the boy, "for I have made a promise not to tell any man or woman."

"Then tell your story to the horse," she said.

The young Lord of Lorn put his arms round the horse's neck and told his story into its ear.

When the Duke's daughter heard what the wicked Steward had done she said she would send a letter to the boy's father to come to him at once.

When the old Lord read the letter both he and his wife were full of sorrow. His mother wept and said,

"I knew what would become of my child in such a far country."

Then the young Lord's father called up all his men and with seven other Lords he set sail for France.

Now the young Lord of Lorn had been taken from the stables and given work as a porter. He had to stand at the gate and open it when anyone came in.

When his father and the seven Lords came riding up to the gate, there was the young Lord of Lorn standing by the door.

At once the Lords dismounted and bowed to their young Lord, while the serving men went down on their knees before him.

When the Steward saw this he cried,

"What men are these, who bow to the porter at the gate?"

"Ah, wicked steward," said the old Lord when he saw him there. "Now you shall die."

The Lords agreed that the wicked Steward should be hanged, and after that his body was put into boiling lead and that was the end of him.

As for the Duke's daughter she said she would marry the young Lord of Lorn. The King of France came to the wedding, bringing a hundred casks of wine with him. Five sets of musicians played music without stopping day or night.

The feasting and singing and dancing went on for nine whole months and never had such a wedding been seen in all the land of France.

Monacella and the Hare

In the mountain country of Wales there once lived a Princess called Monacella. She was kind and gentle and good and everybody loved her. Whenever she heard that any of the people in the village were ill she would go and visit them and take them some warm soup and sit beside them. If the children were unhappy Monacella would talk to them and comfort them, and if ever she found an animal or a bird that was hurt she would take care of it until it was well and then let it go again.

When she was sixteen, her father decided that the time had come for her to marry. There was a Prince in the nearby kingdom who had a splendid castle and many men to fight for him. Monacella's father very much wished her to marry him.

"He will be able to help me fight against my enemies," he said. "And you will always have fine clothes and plenty of servants to wait upon you. You will have all you want."

But this was not what Monacella wanted at all. She did not care about fine clothes and she did not like people fighting one another.

"All I want", she said to herself, "is to live in a quiet place, where people are not cruel to each other, and where I can pray to God."

She saw that her father had made up his mind that she should marry the Prince, so one night Monacella slipped out of the castle and went away into the woods by herself.

She walked and walked until at last she found herself in a lovely valley, green and peaceful. A stream ran through the valley, and nearby Monacella found a little cave.

"This is where I will live," she said, and she knelt down and thanked God for bringing her there.

Then she collected soft moss and bracken and made

herself a bed on the ground in the cave, and there she lived alone, drinking water from the stream and eating the wild berries that grew in the woods.

Before long the people round about found where she was living and she used to visit them and look after their children and the sick people, so that they grew to love her, because she was so kind and good.

They brought her apples and cherries from their gardens, and little cakes they had made for her, and eggs from their hens.

She had other friends too. The birds and the animals that lived in the woods and fields soon came to know that she loved them, and the robins and rabbits and the foxes and blackbirds all came hopping up to her cave to say good morning, and Monacella would smile and say,

"God bless all the animals and birds."

One day, a brown hare came skipping through the valley. It was a lovely morning and the little hare stopped here and there to nibble the green grass. Then he sat up and wriggled his little nose and looked around.

All of a sudden he heard a sound. He laid back his ears and his eyes grew round with fear. It was the sound of a hunting horn and the baying of dogs in the distance. The Lord of the Valley was out hunting.

Away went the little hare, across the field and into the wood. Up and down he ran, through the bushes and out the other side, across the stream and up the hillside, twisting and turning and doubling back, and all the time the sound of the hounds grew nearer and the huntsman's horn came more loud and clear.

"Monacella will save me!" said the hare to himself. "If only I can find her. I must find Monacella!"

And now the hounds were close behind him. He could hear their feet padding on the grass and the thud of the horse's hooves and the cry of the huntsman.

All around him the birds and the little animals were whispering.

"Monacella, Monacella, somebody needs you. Monacella, where are you?"

The little hare made a last dash through the bushes and then he heard a quiet voice,

"God bless all birds and animals." Suddenly it was quiet, and there was Monacella.

A moment after, the Lord of the Valley came riding up on his horse. He pushed his way between the trees, calling his dogs. His horse stepped out into a green clearing and what the huntsman saw made him stand still in amazement.

In the middle of the clearing sat Monacella, her

eyes closed and the hare at her feet, and in a ring around her sat the huntsman's dogs, looking at her.

"We can do nothing," they seemed to be saying, "for she is saying her prayers."

And then a strange thing happened. The Lord of the Valley, as he looked at Monacella, found that he no longer wanted to hunt or kill. Instead he only felt glad that the little hare was safe.

He got down from his horse and spoke to Monacella.

"Dear lady," he said, "for your gentleness and kindness I will give you this valley. It will be a place of safety for all wild things, and no one will ever again hunt or kill so long as you are here."

Then he called up his dogs, and one by one they left the ring and each of them went up to Monacella and wagged his tail and licked her hand. Then quietly they left the clearing with the little hare still sitting there, quite unafraid.

And from that time onwards there was peace in the green valley. Never more was the huntsman's horn heard there, and the birds and animals lived in safety.

The Strange Visitor

In a castle in Wales there lived, long ago, a great Knight, called Sir Laurence Berkrolles. Now, Wales had been captured by the King of England, and Sir Laurence Berkrolles, although he lived in Wales, was a friend of the King. The people of Wales wished their country to be free and at last they rose and fought against the English.

Their leader was a man called Owen Glendower, and the Welsh people gladly followed him into battle.

Owen Glendower recaptured three of the great Welsh castles, but just when it seemed that the English would be driven out of Wales, everything went wrong. Owen Glendower's army was defeated and his son was taken prisoner. Many of the Welsh were killed and their homes burned down.

But Owen Glendower would not give in. He travelled all over Wales, in disguise, trying to raise another Welsh army. Often he travelled with only one man as his companion.

One day two strangers came to the castle of Sir Laurence Berkrolles. They asked if they might speak with Sir Laurence. When they were let in, they said that they were Frenchmen and asked Sir Laurence if they might stay for the night. Sir Laurence said he would be glad for them to stay. He had food brought and they dined together.

After dinner they played a game of chess and one of the strangers sang French songs to Sir Laurence and his Knights.

When they spoke of leaving the next day Sir Laurence said,

"These are troubled times for Wales. It is not safe for you to travel with only one man as a companion. I am told that Owen Glendower is hiding in these parts."

"Indeed," said one of the strangers. "I should like to meet him."

"Well," said Sir Laurence, "if you stay here you

will no doubt do so. My men are searching for him even now. They are sure to take him before long."

The stranger said he would be glad to stay and meet Owen Glendower and so he and his friend remained in the castle for four more days.

At the end of this time he said to Sir Laurence Berkrolles,

"Since your men have not taken Owen Glendower I must stay no longer. I have much to do."

Then he held out his hand, "I give you my hand", he said, "and I thank you for your kindness. I am Owen Glendower!"

Sir Laurence could find no words to say and Owen went on,

"I give you my word, though you are my enemy, that I will never raise my hand in battle against you, nor will I allow any of my people to do so. Let us part friends, and allow me to go in peace."

And so Owen Glendower left the castle.

Sir Laurence Berkrolles kept silent about his strange visitors and the English never knew that their enemy had lived as a friend in the Knight's castle.

Robin Hood and the Silver Arrow

Under a great tree in the forest Robin Hood lay looking up through the leaves at the blue sky. His men sat round in little groups sharpening their arrows and mending their bows and talking to one another.

Suddenly there was a rustling in the leaves, and down the path ran one of the outlaws.

"Master," he called as he came up and threw himself down beside Robin Hood. "I bring news from Nottingham."

"What news?" asked Robin, sitting up, as the other outlaws gathered round to listen.

"The Sheriff of Nottingham is to hold a contest. There is to be a shooting match and the prize is a silver arrow, tipped with gold feathers. The Sheriff has invited all the best archers in the land to take part and he boasts that his own archers will carry off the prize."

"Ha!" cried Robin Hood. "That will never be. We will soon show him who are the best archers. Come, my men, let us get ready and away to Nottingham."

The contest was a trap. The Sheriff of Nottingham, Robin Hood's old enemy, had vowed that he would be rid of Robin, but try as he would he had never been able to catch him.

Time after time he had set out with a band of armed men, to capture Robin Hood. They rode into the forest where Robin and his men lived, but, except for deer and rabbits and the birds in the trees, they found nothing. Robin and his band seemed to vanish into the green shadows, and every time the Sheriff had to return empty handed.

Once, not long before, the Sheriff had seen Robin, but instead of taking him captive, he had himself been caught by the outlaws. Robin Hood had made him stay in the forest and sleep on the ground as the outlaws did. The next day he had let him go free, after the Sheriff had made a promise that he would never harm him. But the Sheriff had no intention of keeping his promise, and was more determined than ever that he would put an end to Robin. How could he get him to come out of the forest, where he was safe?

The Sheriff thought and thought and at last he hit upon the idea of the contest. He knew that Robin would never miss a chance to show his skill as an archer. This, the Sheriff guessed, would bring him from his hiding place.

At last the day came and Robin and his men set off for Nottingham, each with his bow and a fine set of new arrows.

The field where the contest was to be held was just outside the town. At the far end stood the targets, a row of butts painted red and white. Already the archers were lined up to shoot.

Everyone from round about had come to watch and the field was crowded with people trying to get as near as they could and pushing or standing on tiptoe to get a better sight of the contest.

"Whang", went the bows, and "whizz", went the arrows through the air, while the crowd cheered and shouted as the arrows found their marks.

In one corner of the field stood the Sheriff, closely guarded by his armed men. While everybody else was watching the archers, his beady black eyes were scanning the crowd for Robin Hood.

At last he saw him. The last of the Sheriff's own archers had just made his shot, a good one, which brought a cheer from the crowd. He moved back, and into his place stepped a tall man in a green tunic, his head covered by a hood. Pulling an arrow from his belt he set it to his bow, then he threw back his hood.

"Robin Hood! It is Robin Hood!" a whisper went

up from the crowd. Then a great hush fell on everyone as Robin took aim. Straight as a flash of light the arrow flew to the target. "Plung", it went, straight to the bulls-eye.

"He wins! He wins! Robin Hood has won!" yelled the crowd. Caps were thrown into the air as everyone went nearly mad with excitement.

Robin turned to where the Sheriff was standing.

"Come forward and take your prize," the Sheriff ordered.

The crowd made way for Robin as he strode across the green grass. He knelt before the Sheriff to take the silver arrow from his hand and as he did so, the Sheriff called.

"Take him, men! Bind him! Hold him fast!"

But Robin's men were ready. A shower of arrows came flying through the air. The crowd scattered and the Sheriff took to his heels. Before the guards could take him Robin had made his escape and joined the outlaws.

Shooting as they went they made their way across the field, but now the Sheriff had called out the people from the town. With axes, arrows, cudgels, knives and all the weapons they could lay hands on they set off after the band of outlaws.

The forest was still far away but Robin and his men pressed on, turning every so often to shoot a hail of arrows into the crowd that was now close behind them.

Suddenly Robin heard a groan. Down at his feet fell Little John, badly wounded.

"Leave me Master," cried Little John. "Escape yourself, but do not let the Sheriff take me alive. Draw your sword and cut off my head. I beg you!"

"Never!" cried Robin. "We live and die together." Helped by one of the outlaws, he lifted Little John's great weight onto his own back.

On he went, but more slowly now, and every now and then he put Little John on the ground while he shot an arrow at the enemy behind him. Then, lifting him once again, on he went.

The Sheriff's band came closer. Those on horseback were almost on top of the outlaws when, in the nick of time, Robin and his men saw in front of them, a great castle. Robin knew that if only they could reach the castle they would be safe, for it belonged to Sir Richard of the Lea whom Robin had helped not long before.

Once more they stood, a small band close together, raining their arrows into the enemy, and then on again, until they were at the drawbridge. There in the gateway was Sir Richard himself. In less than a moment they were across the drawbridge and up it went behind them. Inside, Sir Richard's men ran to man the walls and throw down stones on the Sheriff's men as they surrounded the castle.

Round the walls galloped the Sheriff's horsemen until the Sheriff, knowing that Robin had escaped him, called them off, and rode back to Nottingham.

As soon as they were safely in the castle Sir Richard's men carefully carried Little John and laid him on a bed, where his wounds were dressed by Sir Richard's lady herself. Then Robin and his men sat down in the great hall. A fine feast was soon provided and great was the merriment as Robin told Sir Richard the story of how he had outwitted the Sheriff once again.

The Siege of Calais

England and France were at war.

Edward, the King of England, had just fought and won a great battle and now he planned to take the town of Calais. But Calais had a great wall all round it, with towers and battlements. The only way in lay through its great gates, but these were closed and armed men guarded the walls, so that the English soldiers could not come near.

Edward knew that the only way to take the town was to keep his army outside the walls and prevent any food being taken inside. In time, the people of Calais would starve and then they would have to give in.

The King made his soldiers build wooden houses all round the walls, where the English army could live until the people of Calais were forced to give in. Here his soldiers stayed, week after week and month after month, until a whole year had gone by.

All this time the people inside the town waited for the King of France to come with his army and save them. But the days and weeks and months went by, and no army came.

Little by little all the food in the town was used up, but the people of Calais refused to give in. They became weaker and weaker through lack of food and at last there was nothing left to eat but the dogs and cats.

The Governor of the town wrote a letter to the King of France telling him all that was happening to them and begging him to come to their rescue. At last one bright morning, the watchman on the walls saw, far away, the glint of sunlight on the spears and helmets of a great army.

"We are saved! We are saved!" cried the people.

"The King is coming at last to save us!" They ran to the walls to watch the army riding closer.

The King of France set up his camp and the people waited anxiously for him to attack the army of England, but nothing happened. There was no sound of battle and no clash of arms. Days passed, but no battle took place. Instead, the King of France tried to make peace with Edward of England.

Then one morning the watchman on the walls saw a sad sight. As he watched he saw the army of France moving away, and soon its banners and spears and horsemen vanished in the distance. Calais was left with no hope of rescue. When the Governor saw that all hope had gone he sadly climbed up to the walls, carrying a white flag. From the battlements he looked down on the English army camped below. Holding the flag high above his head he waved it, and when the English soldiers saw it they knew that Calais was ready to give itself up.

The King of England at once sent two of his knights to speak with the Governor. The guards let them into the town and they were taken before the Governor.

"We must give in," he said. "We have no food left. We will yield to your King if he will spare our lives." The knights returned to the King of England and told him what the Governor had said. But Edward, after waiting a whole year, was angry that they should ask him to spare their lives.

"They shall all die," he said. "Go back and tell them the King of England makes no terms."

But the knights, who had been inside the city and seen the starving people, knew how brave they were, and they begged the King to show mercy.

At last Edward said,

"This I will do. If the Governor will send me six of the greatest men of the town, the rest shall go free. But they must come to me bareheaded and with ropes around their necks and bring me the keys of the castle and the town."

One of the knights then returned to the Governor and gave him the King's message. At once the Governor went to the market place and told the bellman to ring the great bell to call all the people together.

When they had all come to the market place the Governor sorrowfully told them what King Edward had said. As he had finished speaking a great silence fell upon everyone. Who would be brave enough to offer himself to save the town? After a long moment, a man stepped out of the crowd.

"I will go," he said quietly.

He stood there alone for a few moments, then another man stepped out and stood beside him.

"And I will go with you," he said.

Then another joined them, and another and another, until there were six men standing in the market place, six of the greatest men of Calais, ready to give themselves up to save the townspeople.

Ropes were put round their necks and then, barefooted and bareheaded, they walked to the great gate which had been shut for a whole year.

Carrying the keys of the town and the castle, they made their way out to the English camp and into the King's tent. There they knelt down and offered the keys to Edward.

The King looked down at them and said,

"Take them away and cut off their heads."

The knights begged him to have mercy.

"These men have come and given themselves to you to save the lives of the townspeople," they said. "Such a brave deed should not be punished, but rewarded."

But the King would not listen to them.

"They shall be put to death," he said.

Now the Queen, whose name was Philippa, was there in the tent beside Edward. When she saw how brave the six men were, she fell on her knees in front of him.

"Have mercy," she said. "I have never asked anything of you before, but now I beg you, by your love for me, let these men go."

The King looked at her, without speaking. Then he tried to make her rise from her knees, but she stayed

kneeling in front of him, until at last he said, "I can refuse you nothing. Take them and do with them as you please."

The ropes were taken off their necks and they were dressed in new clothes. Then Queen Philippa made a great feast for the six men and after they had eaten she sent them back, with gifts of food and money.

With great joy the people welcomed them back and so, at last, by means of six brave men and a good Queen, the siege of Calais was at an end.

Richard the Lion Heart

Richard the Lion Heart, the King of England, was returning from the Holy Land where he had been fighting the Turks.

As his ship sailed towards home there was a great storm. The ship was driven onto the rocks and wrecked.

Almost everyone on the ship was drowned but the King escaped with a few of his knights. The land on which the ship was wrecked belonged to the Duke of Austria. Richard and the Duke were enemies and the King knew that his life would be in danger if he was captured, so he and his knights dressed up as merchants.

More than once they were nearly captured and after many adventures Richard was at last left with one knight and a page.

For days they had been travelling, not daring to show themselves openly, and were tired and hungry. At last they came to a town. Richard and the knight hid themselves while the page went to buy food.

The King gave the page a bag of gold and off he went into the town.

He found his way to the market place where he bought food, but when the merchant saw the piece of gold he gave in payment he looked at him and said,

"Who is your master?"

"My master is a merchant travelling home from the Holy Land," said the page.

The man looked at him again and then he saw that the page was carrying a pair of fine gloves in his belt, decorated with silver and gold. In those days only rich men wore gloves and these were such that only a prince or a king would have.

One of the men standing by grabbed them from the page's belt.

"A merchant is he?" he cried. "These are king's gloves. Tell us, boy, who is your master?"

Bravely the page stood his ground and said,

"He is a merchant as I told you."

By now a crowd had gathered and they began to beat the page to try to make him tell who his master really was, but the page said nothing.

Then they took him away to the Palace of the Duke of Austria and told the Duke all that happened. The Duke had him beaten and cruelly treated until, at last, the poor page was made to say who his master really was.

When the Duke heard that Richard the Lion Heart was in his country and not far away he sent men to find his hiding place. They took him, put him in prison and kept him there until the Duke sold him to the Emperor of Germany for a great sum of money.

The Emperor put Richard in a secret prison in Germany, telling no one where he was.

All the people of England were sad when Richard did not return to them. His brother told them that Richard was dead and that he was to be their king, but the people did not love Richard's brother and they did not believe what he said.

There was one man who made up his mind to try to find his king and master. This was Blondel, a minstrel. All alone he set out, taking his harp with him. How was he to find the King? Blondel knew that if only Richard could hear him singing, he would sing too, wherever he was.

From castle to castle he wandered, through the length and breadth of Germany. Outside each castle he stood under the walls and played his harp and sang, but no voice came from within to answer him.

Blondel began to grow tired and sad. It seemed a hopeless task that he had taken on.

At last, one evening, he came to a great castle. Standing under the dark walls he took his harp and began to sing once more. He came to the end of the first verse and stopped for a moment to listen. To his great joy he heard a man's voice, a voice he knew, singing the next verse of the song. It was Richard the Lion Heart. Blondel's journey was over. He had found the King.

He made haste back to England to tell the people he had found Richard, but that the Emperor of Germany would not let him go until England paid him a great sum of money.

The people of England wanted so much to have Richard back that, in time, they collected the money that was needed. And so, at last, after his long years of captivity, Richard the Lion Heart came home to England.

Over the Sea to Skye

A mist lay over the mountains and a soft rain fell from the grey sky. Down in the heather a man lay hiding. He had been there all day and now he was stiff and cold from the wet. The hills and glens all around were full of soldiers, all searching for him.

It was Bonnie Prince Charlie of Scotland. He had fought his last battle against the English. His army had been defeated and he himself had escaped. Now he was a hunted man.

The King of England had promised a large sum of money to anyone who would give him away, but Bonnie Prince Charlie had many friends among the mountains and glens of Scotland. Instead of betraying him they gave him food and helped to hide him. The soldiers, however, were never far away and it was not safe for him to stay anywhere for long.

At last he reached the coast and here some friends smuggled him on board a small boat to take him to one of the islands. The night was stormy and the sea rough, but at last they reached land. From one hiding place to another the Prince went, sometimes walking or running through the heather, sometimes going by boat along the coast, shabbily dressed, cold and hungry and often soaked through with the rain. But Prince Charles was strong and brave and used to hardship and living in the open air.

At length he came to a hut on the side of a hill where he lived for three weeks. Higher up the hill, above the hut, there was a cave to which Charles used to climb and look down over the sea. Below, on the water, he saw the boats of his enemies searching for him.

His friends knew where he was and they came to him, bringing him food and news of the movements of the soldiers. One night, one of them came creeping up to the hut under cover of darkness, with some bad news.

"The soldiers are coming here," he said. "They are going to land and take you prisoner. You must make haste and escape to Skye."

Skye was another island off the coast of Scotland, where it was thought that he would be safe. When the Prince heard the news he and two of his friends at once set out across the heather.

In another hut on the side of one of the island hills a young woman lay sleeping. Her name was Flora Macdonald. That day she had taken her brother's cows up on to the hillside to feed.

Suddenly she was awakened by someone beside her in the hut. She sat up in the moonlight and looked into the face of a man. It was one of the Prince's friends.

"The Prince is outside," he said. "He wishes to speak to you."

Flora threw on some clothes and went outside. The Prince stayed hidden behind the hut while Flora was told of the plan to save him.

This was it: Flora was to go to Skye, to visit her

mother and she was to take the Prince with her, disguised as her maid.

Flora knew how dangerous such an adventure would be and she begged not to have to take it on. But the Prince himself appeared from the shadows behind the hut and the three men and Flora stood talking on the hillside with the moon shining on the sea below them. The Prince begged Flora to help him.

He told her that she need have no fear and so, at last, she agreed to the plan. She brought the Prince a bowl of cream and together they planned a meeting place. Then Flora gave the men some bread and cheese to take with them and they slipped away in the moonlight, leaving her alone once more.

Next day Flora set out for the secret meeting place. On the way she found the road barred by soldiers. They demanded to see her passport and then they took her prisoner.

Meanwhile Charles and his two friends lay hidden in the heather, eating the bread and cheese that Flora had given them and keeping watch for soldiers. They had been there most of the day when a man appeared, slipping quietly through the heather. As he came he kept looking behind him to see if he was being followed.

He dropped to his knees beside them in their hiding place.

"I come from Flora Macdonald," he said. "She tells me to say all is well, but the fords over the rivers are all guarded by soldiers and you will not be able to pass."

"I will go and see," said one of the Prince's friends and at once he set out.

It was as the messenger had said.

When the Prince's friend reached the ford across the river he found it guarded and, in a moment, he, too, was a prisoner.

Next morning he was taken before the Captain and there he found Flora.

The Captain was Flora's stepfather. As soon as the soldiers had brought her to him she told him the whole story. When he had heard what she planned to do the Captain let both the prisoners go free and to help her, in case she was stopped again, he gave Flora a letter. The letter was to her mother and it said,

"I have sent your daughter from this country, lest she should be in any way frightened with the troops lying here. She has got one, Betty Burke, an Irish girl, who is a good spinner. If her spinning pleases you, you can keep her till she spins all your lint, or if you have any wool to spin, you may employ her."

Betty Burke was to be the Prince himself.

The next problem was to find some clothes for him to wear. Flora went to a house of a friend, Lady Clan, who she knew would help, but the Prince was tall and there were no clothes in the house big enough for him. All that night the servants sat up making a dress and other clothes for him.

In the meantime the Prince, with two of his friends, made their way over the moors in a gale of driving rain and wind. Soaked to the skin and shivering with cold they reached a hut belonging to a farmer and his wife, who took them in.

Early next morning the farmer's wife woke them up.

"The soldiers will be coming any moment to buy milk," she said. "You must leave at once."

It was still raining and the three friends set off towards the shore, where they tried to find shelter under the rocks. One of them set off to take a message to Flora.

When they thought that it was safe the Prince and the friend who was left with him returned to the farm where they were given some milk to drink, and here the Prince spent the night. He slept on an old door, wrapped in his wet cloak, and covered with a sail.

At last the Betty Burke clothes were ready and Flora and Lady Clan set out to take them to him. While they were gone the General of the army that

was trying to find Charles came to Lady Clan's house.

When he found she was not there he commanded that she be found and brought back, and a messenger was sent to find her.

When Lady Clan heard what had happened she set off for home. What should she say to the General? If he guessed where she had been, the Prince would be lost. At last she thought of a story and by the time she reached home she knew what she would say.

The General at once sent for her and, as she expected, he asked her where she had been.

"I have been to visit a sick child," she said, but the General did not believe her. He asked her the child's name and where it lived, but he could not make her change her story and at last, unable to find out anything, he and his soldiers went away.

Meanwhile the Prince put on the clothes that Flora had brought for him, a white linen dress sprigged with blue, a quilted petticoat, a cap and apron and a cloak with a hood. The Prince wanted to take his pistols under his dress, but Flora would not let him, in case he was searched. But he did take a short heavy cudgel to knock down anyone who should attack him.

When the Prince was ready, all they had to do was to await the boat that was to take them to Skye. The Prince, disguised as Betty Burke, lit a fire on the rocks to warm them while they waited.

At last they saw a boat coming towards the shore, followed by four more. They could see that the boats were full of soldiers.

Quickly Charles and Flora put out the fire and ran to hide in the heather. With beating hearts they watched and, to their great relief, the boats sailed on without stopping. The soldiers had not seen them.

Evening came on and in the twilight they saw another boat slip out from its hiding place. It was the one that was to take them to Skye. It drew in to the shore, and Flora and the Prince climbed in. At first the sea was calm, but about midnight a gale began to blow. The rain came down and a thick mist spread across the sea so that they could see nothing. The Prince began to sing and at last Flora, who had been very much afraid, fell asleep.

As morning came the rain stopped but there was a strong wind blowing so that the rowers could hardly keep the boat moving. At last they came in sight of the island and were about to go ashore when they saw a group of men on the beach. They were soldiers keeping watch. When they saw the boat some of them ran to tell their Captain. The rowers in the Prince's boat pulled hard on their oars, heading for some high rocks. Luckily the tide was low so that the soldiers

could not easily get their boat into the water, and before they were able to follow them the Prince and his friends had turned in to the shelter of a cove, where they were hidden.

When they felt it was safe, they again put out to sea and rowed until they came to another part of the island.

Leaving the Prince in the boat, Flora and one of the men went to seek help from Lady Margaret, a friend of Flora's. Quickly they made their way to the house, but as they drew near they met a servant coming towards them.

"The officers are in the house," she said, "and the soldiers are out searching the countryside for the Prince."

Flora hurried on to the house and, keeping out of the way of the soldiers, she found Lady Margaret alone.

Here she told her all the story. What were they to do? The Prince was on the very doorstep and the house was full of the officers and soldiers of the enemy. To gain time to think, Lady Margaret sent Flora to speak to one of the officers. She was to keep him talking while Lady Margaret worked out a plan.

The officer was pleased to see Flora and while she kept him talking, Lady Margaret sent someone to find the Prince and take him somewhere for the night where he would be safe.

But it was too dangerous for him to stay on the island of Skye any longer. Somehow he must get away. The Prince was told to go to another secret place where a boat, under the cover of darkness, would come to take him away.

Next morning, still disguised as Betty Burke, the Prince set out with a boy to guide him across the hills. When they had gone some distance the Prince went into a wood and took off his woman's clothes. He put on a kilt and jacket and cloak and carefully hid the Betty Burke clothes under a rock.

Meanwhile Flora set out, on horseback, to meet him. Evening came and the Prince and Flora both reached the inn which was the secret meeting place. They had supper together, and just as they had finished, a messenger arrived.

"The boat is here and ready," he said.

The Prince said farewell to Flora and then, in the dark and rain, he went down to the shore. Here the boat was waiting for him and as dawn broke over the grey sea, the Prince stepped on board. The little boat set off across the water, bearing him to safety. Prince Charles had escaped once more.

Grace Darling

The coast of Northumberland is a wild and lonely place where the seas are always cold. Strong north east winds blow across the water, whipping it up in gales and storms, across the shifting sand dunes and stunted trees.

On a rocky island off the coast there stood a lighthouse. All through the long night its light could be seen across the dark sea, warning the ships not to come too close to the rocks where they might be dashed to pieces.

The keeper of the lighthouse, William Darling, with his wife and daughter, Grace, were the only people living on the island. Every evening they climbed up the winding staircase to the top of the lighthouse and lit the oil lantern. Then Grace and her father took it in turn to watch, to make sure the lantern did not go out, and to look out for passing ships.

One night Grace had gone to bed, leaving her father on watch. Some time before midnight the wind went round to the north and turned to a gale. The storm lashed the water round the foot of the lighthouse and the wind roared and howled round the lantern. In the early hours of the morning William Darling woke his daughter to help him. She dressed herself and climbed down the winding stair.

Her father opened the lighthouse door which led on to the rock.

A great gust of wind caught the door, almost pulling it out of his hands. The spray from the huge waves breaking over the rock blew into their faces as they struggled over the slippery rock to where their boat was tied.

Grace's hands were stiff with the cold but she helped her father to fasten the ropes more firmly. They took inside anything that might be washed away.

When all was safe Mr. Darling went to bed, leaving Grace to watch.

The dark hours passed slowly and then just before dawn, as the sky began to grow light, Grace, looking out from the lantern, saw a dark shape, close to the rocks.

It was a ship, or rather, what was left of a ship, for the rest of it had gone down. Grace knew that it must have struck the rocks and at once she went below to wake her father.

William Darling arose and climbed up to the lantern. He looked through the telescope to the wreck to see if there was anyone aboard, but it was still dark and the waves were breaking over what was left of the ship so that he could not see clearly.

Slowly it grew light and the tide went down and, at last, about two hours later, Grace saw three or four men on the rocks.

The Darling's boat was tied below but it was heavy and needed three men to row it. Could Grace and her father do it alone? If they could manage to reach the rock through the heavy seas it would be even more difficult and dangerous coming back, for the tide would be against them. But if they could get some of the men off the rock they would have some help for the return journey.

Grace's mother begged them not to go, but when she saw that nothing would stop them she helped them to get out the boat and then climbed up to the lantern to watch.

Standing by the window Mrs. Darling looked out over the running sea. Where was the boat with Grace and her father in it? She could not see it. Thinking it had been overturned with the waves, she fainted. When she came to she looked through the telescope and there, to her joy, she saw the boat, heading for the distant rocks on which the ship had been wrecked.

The Darling's boat drew closer to the rock and now Grace could see that there were nine people there, eight men and one woman. As they rowed nearer, the survivors began to crowd down to the edge of the rock to get into the boat.

At once Mr. Darling jumped out to hold them, for he could only take five at one time. Grace, cold to the bone and wet with sea water, held the boat as still as she could against the wash of the waves and the gale. The lives of ten people would be lost if she let go, but her courage did not fail, and one by one, four of the men and the woman were taken on board. The rest had to stay behind on the rock and wait for the boat to return. Now there were men to help row and William Darling and three of them took an oar each and began the long journey back to the lighthouse.

Two of the men returned with Mr. Darling to fetch the rest of the survivors off the rock, and at last, thanks to the courage of Grace and her father, they were all safely landed at the lighthouse.

Back from Space—
The Story of Apollo 13

Three men were on their way to the Moon. All was going well. Apollo 11, a few months before, had safely landed the first men to walk on the Moon. It had gone perfectly. Millions of people had seen it all on their television sets, the blast off, the perfect flight towards the Moon and the landing of the Lunar Module. They had seen the two men get out and walk on the Moon for the first time in history. Safely, without a hitch, the rocket had returned to Earth and the splashdown in the Pacific Ocean. Now it looked as though the journey of Apollo 13 would be just as perfect.

The rocket was three days out in space, three hundred and thirty thousand kilometres from Earth. Then, when all seemed to be going well, something happened.

It was Monday, April 13th, when suddenly the voice of one of the astronauts, Jack Swigert, was heard over the radio. "Hey," he said, "we've got a problem here." From this moment all was changed, and the world was gripped with suspense, which was to last for three and a half days.

Help was at once offered from many countries, while the men in Mission Control set about the task of doing all they could to save the three men.

Aboard the rocket, flashing lights and an alarm on the instrument panel told the astronauts that something was wrong, but they did not know what it was. Now the voice of the leading astronaut, James Lovell, came through.

"We've had a problem," he said. "We've had a main B – bus interval."

This was the astronaut's way of saying that there had been a loss of electric power. This was what had set off the alarm and the flashing lights.

In less than a minute came the voice of the co-pilot, Fred Haise.

"We had a pretty large bang," he said.

The men at Mission Control now found something even worse than the loss of power. The supply of oxygen gas was failing.

"It looks to me", came Lovell's voice over the radio, "that we're venting something out into space. It's a gas of some sort."

Now the men at Mission Control knew that there had been an explosion in the rocket, but just what had happened and how much damage had been done, nobody could tell.

All they knew was that the rocket must be brought back to earth as quickly as possible, and that every minute counted.

At this stage the astronauts were heading towards the Moon at a speed of about three thousand kilometres an hour. Could the rocket be guided back to Earth quickly enough before the electrical power, the oxygen and the water ran out?

About an hour after the explosion the astronauts reported that the power was still failing. At last Fred Haise called on the radio,

"I don't have any current now. Hey! It's off, it's off."

One of the two oxygen tanks was useless and it seemed that the second one was damaged too. It was clear that some damage had taken place in the Service Module. The only way now was for the astronauts to use the Lunar Module to get them home.

The Lunar Module had been intended for the landing on the Moon, but now it was to be used as a lifeboat in space. It had its own rocket engines and electricity, water and oxygen and the astronauts' lives would depend on whether or not everything would work.

Lovell and Haise climbed into the Lunar Module and switched on the electricity and oxygen while Swigert stayed in the Command Module.

Now the rocket had to be guided on to a different path from the one on which it was travelling.

This was to be done by firing the rocket engines in the Lunar Module. No one could be sure if the engines would fire or not. If they did not, or if anything else went wrong, the rocket would travel on into outer space, missing the Earth by more than six thousand kilometres.

Meanwhile the whole world waited in suspense. Men, women and children prayed. Special services were held in thousands of churches.

Early on Tuesday morning, April 14th, James Lovell set to work to fire the engine in the Lunar Module.

Mission Control waited in silent suspense. Would it work? They had less than a minute to wait and then they knew that the rockets had fired and now the spaceship was on a new path.

So far, all was well and Lovell took the first watch with Swigert, while Haise climbed back into the Command Module to get some sleep. About six hours later they changed places, leaving Haise alone on watch in the Lunar Module. Meanwhile, on Earth, the work of rescue went on, while other astronauts did all they could to help the wives and families of the men in Apollo 13.

If the spaceship came safely back to Earth, where would it land? The plan had been for the splashdown to take place in the Pacific, but now nobody could be sure the space ship would be guided there. Plans were made for rescue in three oceans, the Pacific, the Atlantic and the Indian Ocean.

On Tuesday evening the rocket stage that had launched the spaceship on its way crashed into the Moon like a gigantic bomb.

The time came for the second firing of the rockets to change the path of the spaceship so that it would

land in the Pacific, but now there was a new difficulty. The air in the cabin had become stale and it grew very cold inside the spaceship. Lovell radioed to Mission Control.

"Jack and Fred are going to sleep. Fred's sleeping place is now in the tunnel, upside down, with his head resting on the engine cover. Jack is on the floor of the Lunar Module with a harness around his arm to keep him there."

But it was too cold to sleep and the men became tired and irritable. There were still three days to go, with the most dangerous part of the journey still to come. The spaceship had to pass through the Earth's atmosphere before it could splash down in the ocean. Would it burn up as it entered the atmosphere or would it be strong enough to withstand the great heat? Nobody knew. The Lunar Module was not strong enough for this and the Service Module was useless. Would the Command Module bring the astronauts safely home?

On Friday morning the Service Module was cast off. For the first time since they left Earth, six days before, the astronauts were able to see the Service Module. They were shocked at what they saw. A whole panel had been blown out.

Lovell's voice came over the radio,

"There's one whole side of that space craft missing," he said. "It looks like the explosion stained it, a dark brown streak. It's really a mess."

Now there was only one hour left before the spaceship was to enter the Earth's atmosphere. Lovell and Haise left the Lunar Module and climbed through the tunnel into the Command Module. They closed the hatches and filled the tunnel with oxygen, then they moved the switches which would cast off the Lunar Module.

"Farewell," radioed Mission Control to the Lunar Module as it shot away, "and we thank you."

Now there were sixteen thousand kilometres still to go. Suspense was still high in Mission Control. No one knew if the Command Module had been damaged as well as the Service Module. No one could be sure if it would come safely through the atmosphere or not.

An hour after the Lunar Module had been cast off, the Command Module plunged into the atmosphere over the Pacific, and the last and most dangerous part of the journey had started. For now there was no way of knowing what was happening in the spaceship.

Once it had entered the atmosphere the radio messages stopped. All was silence. No voices from the astronauts. No messages. No reports.

For six minutes there was silence, while the world held its breath. What was happening out there? Would the spaceship ever be seen again? Would the astronauts come home, or would it end in disaster and tragedy?

At last the long minutes of waiting were over, and the spaceship was seen, dropping gently down out of the clouds, hanging below its three great parachutes. A deep sigh of relief and thankfulness went up from the millions of people watching their television screens all over the world.

The Command Module came down in the Pacific Ocean and the astronauts were taken out and carried safe and well by helicopter to the waiting ship.

Next day, the President of the United States

himself flew out to present medals to the three astronauts.

"You did not reach the moon," he said to them, "but you reached the hearts of millions of people on Earth by what you did."

Notes

In this book the children should be able to recognise the following, examples of which have appeared in the earlier Silver Books:

“air” as in armchair, e.g. Lothaire.
“oar” as in roar, e.g. board, oars.
“our” as in armour, e.g. courage.
“ure” as in furniture, e.g. adventure.

New words 8

Page	
5	island
23	quoit(s)
46	Eng(land) (lish)
57	Calais
70	Skye
91	’ve (as in we’ve)
	minute(s)
	’s (as in it’s, there’s)

All other words have appeared in earlier books or can be built, using the phonic rules learned so far.